KEEP KEEP

CALM CALM

FOR FOR

AUSSIES AUSSIES

KEEP KEEP

CALM CALM

FOR FOR

AUSSIES AUSSIES

KEEP KEEP

CALM CALM

FOR FOR

AUSSIES AUSSIES

KEEP CALM FOR AUSSIES

KEEP CALM FOR AUSSIES
KEEP CALM FOR AUSSIES
KEEP CALM FOR AUSSIES
KEEP CALM FOR AUSSIES
KEEP CALM FOR AUSSIES
KEEP CALM FOR AUSSIES
KEEP CALM FOR AUSSIES

KEEP
CALM
FOR
AUSSIES

KEEP CALM FOR AUSSIES

With research by Madeleine Stevens

Summersdale Publishers Ltd
46 West Street
Chichester
West Sussex
PO19 1RP
UK

www.summersdale.com

Printed and bound in China

ISBN: 978-1-84953-866-4

Substantial discounts on bulk quantities of Summersdale books are available to corporations, professional associations and other organisations. For details contact Nicky Douglas by telephone: +44 (0) 1243 756902, fax: +44 (0) 1243 786300 or email: nicky@summersdale.com.

KEEP
CALM
FOR
AUSSIES

summersdale

Australia is, properly speaking, an island, but it is… classed as a continent in order to convey to the mind a just idea of its magnitude.

Charles Sturt

Even the Australians
don't know how
beautiful their
own country is.

Brian Cox

His kangaroo is loose
in the top paddock.

**Australian saying, meaning that
someone is not very bright – or
even mad**

Australians have a free
spirit and an ability to
think outside the box.

Brian Schmidt

There is a long-running dispute between Australia and New Zealand over which country invented the popular meringue-based dessert, the pavlova. It's thought that it was named in honour of Anna Pavlova, the Russian ballerina. *The Oxford English Dictionary* traced the first recorded pavlova recipe to New Zealand, but the fierce debate continues…

I can't think of a nobler
description of anybody
than to be called an
average Australian bloke.

John Howard

Beer makes you feel
the way you ought to
feel without beer.

Henry Lawson

To drink with the flies.

Australian saying, meaning to drink alone

Those who lose dreaming are lost.

Aboriginal proverb

Australia is, in fact, the other side of that fence.

Douglas Adams on the grass being greener in Australia

sence of Australia is our lack of sophistication – our refusal to conform to pretension and superficiality.

Tim Macartney-Snape

With Australians we're
saying we're going to
win before we start
playing and pretty much
keep on saying that.

Shane Warne

Morning: Slept.
Afternoon: Slept.
Evening: Ate grass.
Night: Ate grass.
Decided grass is boring.
Scratched… Slept.

Jackie French, *Diary of a Wombat*

Wombat poo is cube-shaped!
The poop successfully marks
out a wombat's territory since
it does not easily get moved
from, or roll off, wherever it is
deposited, such as along the tops
of branches and on leaves.

Obstacles are there to
get around, climb over
or scramble through.

Pat O'Shane

Courage.

**The motto of the Australian
Army's 2nd Cavalry Regiment**

People who say 'There's nothing to fear from spiders' have clearly never been to Australia.

Cate Blanchett

A sense of humour
is just common
sense, dancing.

Clive James

Friendship is
warmth in cold;
firm ground in a bog.

Miles Franklin

Reconciliation requires changes of heart and spirit, as well as social and economic change. It requires symbolic as well as practical action.

Malcolm Fraser

Australian humour. It's
different and baked
by a bigger sun.

Anonymous

In 2006, a man from Brisbane
tried to sell New Zealand on
eBay at a starting price of $0.01.
When the auction was closed
after thousands of hits and 22 bids,
the selling price had reached $3,000.
New Zealand's Minister for
Foreign Affairs was not amused.

If better is possible,
good is not enough.

George Furner Langley

The bigger the hat, the smaller the property.

Australian proverb

Kylie Minogue is the greatest
thing that has happened
to Australian music.

Nick Cave

We were a country full of sheep and convicts.

Geoffrey Rush on the British view of Australia in the 1970s

To be the best you
have to beat the best.

Ryan Carneli

Disappointment and
adversity can be catalysts
for greatness.

Cathy Freeman

There is nothing
more Australian than
our commitment
to 'a fair go'.

Malcolm Turnbull

Our world is a web of interdependencies woven so tightly it sometimes becomes love.

Tim Flannery, *Here on Earth*

Although mining is one of
Australia's most important
industries, only 0.26 per cent of
the land mass is used for mines.
More land is taken up by pubs.

Out in the bush, the
tarred road always ends
just after the house
of the local mayor.

Australian proverb

In the field of snobbery,
Australia is an
underdeveloped country.

George Mikes

Australians are
coffee snobs.

Hugh Jackman

Australian Rules
football might best
be described as a
game devised for
padded cells, played
in the open air.

James Murray, *Remembrance of
Things Australian*

You know you're in
Melbourne when you're
walking through the park
and you see someone
kicking the footy with
cricket pads on.

Hung Le

Vocal adjustments
are needed to reduce
the bloody velocity
of words in the wide
spaces of Orstraliah.

Murray Bail, *Homesickness*

The food is excellent. The beer is cold. The sun nearly always shines. Life doesn't get much better than this.

Bill Bryson, *In a Sunburned Country*

There is healing in
our dreams. Let us
dare to dream again.

Ted Lovett

The very first gathering of Labor members took place underneath a gum tree in Barcaldine, Queensland, in 1891. Though the 'Tree of Knowledge', as it has been named, may be apocryphal, it highlights the party's rural roots in the Great Shearers' Strike – one of the country's earliest industrial disputes.

Never be afraid to
laugh at yourself,
after all, you could
be missing out on the
joke of the century.

**Barry Humphries aka
Dame Edna Everage**

Australians don't have a preconceived notion of what things have to be… we can go on a fantastic journey.

Yahoo Serious

In the race of life, always
back self-interest; at least
you know it's trying.

Jack Lang

Life is a boomerang.
What you give, you
get right back.

Anonymous

A fart competing
with thunder.

**Graham Gooch on the
1990–91 Ashes**

With just about every player in Australia, his whole goal and ambition is to play for Australia… It's just a different attitude.

Shane Warne on first-class cricket

If you find an Australian indoors, it's a fair bet that he will have a glass in his hand.

Jonathan Aitken

Neighbours, the renowned Aussie soap opera, celebrated its thirtieth anniversary in 2015. There's never a dull moment, with 15 births, 41 marriages, 35 deaths and counting.

Follow your dreams…
If you have enough
determination you
will get there.

Sally Morgan

How do you navigate
around Australia in a
16-foot boat? You just keep
Australia on the left.

Hans Tholstrup

Queensland:
beautiful one day,
perfect the next.

Queensland slogan

If Paris is a city of lights, Sydney is the city of fireworks.

Baz Luhrmann

Success isn't final.
Failure isn't fatal. It's
courage that counts.

Alicia Coutts

Give it a crack and
see what happens.

Anh Do

Any boss who sacks
anyone for not turning
up today is a bum.

**Bob Hawke, prime minister at the
time, after the historic victory of
the yacht *Australia II* in the 1983
America's Cup**

A platypus is a
duck designed by
a committee.

Anonymous

Should you decide to visit a different Australian beach every single day, you would need to set aside over 27 years of your life – perhaps this should come as no surprise when you consider that the mainland has 35,000 kilometres of coastline and the islands another 23,000 kilometres.

The beach, in Australia, is the landscape equivalent of the veranda, a veranda at the edge of the continent.

Tim Winton, *Land's Edge*

The secret to my success
is that I bit off more than
I could chew and chewed
as fast as I could.

Paul Hogan

As tough as a ute
load of mallee roots.

Australian saying

Australia has always
encouraged the little
bloke to have a go, the
Aussie battler to get up.

Andrew Forrest

Act quickly,
think slowly.

Germaine Greer

The lovely thing
about being 40 is that
you can appreciate
25-year-old men more.

Colleen McCullough

*The Australian Book
of Etiquette* is a
very slim volume.

Paul Theroux

Bob Hawke achieved notoriety – and made it into *Guinness World Records* – when, as a Rhodes scholar at Oxford University in 1954, he drank a yard glass of ale in under 12 seconds. He later became prime minister of Australia and governed the amber-nectar-loving country.

Australians don't
take themselves
too seriously.

Naomi Watts

I can't go without
Vegemite.

Phoebe Tonkin

The time your game is
most vulnerable is when
you're ahead; never let up.

Rod Laver

I'm interested in where we
are, where we're going,
where we've come from.

Peter Carey

May as well be here,
we are as where we are.

Aboriginal proverb

Well may we say
'God save the Queen',
because nothing will save
the Governor-General.

**Gough Whitlam on hearing that
he was the first Australian prime
minister to be dismissed**

It's nice to put your hand up and do the big things the team requires of you.

Ricky Ponting

The moment is
your only duty.

Barry Long, *Knowing Yourself*

Per ardua ad astra.
Through struggle
to the stars.

RAAF motto

The Australian company Quiksilver
is one of the largest surf-wear
manufacturers in the world.
Now based in California, it was
started in 1969 in Belles Beach, west
of Melbourne. Its logo was inspired
by Hokusai's woodcut of a wave.
Rip Curl, another surf-wear
company, was founded on the same
surf beach in the same year.

God bless America.
God save the Queen.
God defend New Zealand
and thank Christ for Australia.

Russell Crowe

Aussie slang

Arvo – afternoon

Bonzer (bonza) – great

Cactus – broken

Fair dinkum – genuine

Hit the turps – to go drinking

No worries – no problem

Ridgy-didge – genuine

('ridge' is an old slang term for 'gold' or 'real')

She'll be right – it'll be OK

Too right – definitely

You've got Buckley's –

you've got no chance

(this originates from a Melbourne shop,

Buckley's and Nunn, which is how this

phrase came to mean 'no chance at all')

When you play Test cricket, you don't give the Englishmen an inch.

Donald Bradman

You can do anything
if you believe
in yourself.

Marjorie Jackson-Nelson

Matches are won and
lost so many times
in the locker room.

Lleyton Hewitt

You can be tops in
Australia and be unheard
of anywhere else.

Barry Gibb

Male lyrebirds uncannily mimic human sounds such as car alarms, chainsaws and camera shutters. They also imitate other birdcalls in the pursuit of mates and their voices can travel up to one kilometre through the rainforest.

Australia is about
as far away as you
can get. I like that.

André 3000

A lot of my identity as
an Aboriginal person
is about family.

Shari Sebbens

Australians are
just British people
who are happy.

Craig Hill

What beefsteak is to Argentina, flamenco to Spain… what money is to a Swiss, that is outdoor-life to an Australian.

George Mikes

I was fair-skinned
in a country that's
about the outdoors.

Nicole Kidman

To win in Australia, for me, has to be the ultimate success because the Aussies live for sport.

Ian Botham

If the Poms bat
first, let's tell the
taxi to wait.

Australian fans' banner

Selfies originated in Australia!
In 2001, Australians uploaded
self-taken group photos to the
internet for the first time. It was an
Australian student, known as Hopey,
who coined the word 'selfie' in 2002.

When [Australians] see the face of disaster... they joke with it and shake its hand.

Donald Horne, *Southern Exposure*

We are all one blood.
No matter where we
are from, we are all
one blood, the same.

David Gulpilil

Marvellous.

**Richie Benaud's trademark
word for describing
something he admired**

It is extremely difficult...
to convey to one who
has not visited Sydney
any adequate idea of the
beauties of its scenery.

Anthony Trollope

While Sydney and Melbourne fight about who wears Australia's cultural crown, Canberra just gets on with it.

Judy Horacek

I have learned to not worry
about things I can't control.

Jay Weatherill

Sent off, carried off,
but never backed off.

**David Dunworth on playing
rugby union**

At 3.00 p.m. on the first Tuesday of November, the nation stops to watch a 3,200-metre race for three-year-old thoroughbred horses at Melbourne's Flemington Racecourse. The Melbourne Cup is such an institution that it went ahead during both world wars, even though most major sporting events were stopped during wartime.

At the end of my trial,
I was rather hoping
the judge would send
me to Australia for
the rest of my life.

Jeffrey Archer

Sport is one of the pillars of
the Australian way of life.

John Howard

Australian cricketers
just love tradition.

Matthew Hayden

Where I live if someone
gives you a hug it's
from the heart.

Steve Irwin

Big things are often
just small things
that are noticed.

Markus Zusak

Dog must not
steal from dog.

Convict saying

It's a sign of your own
worth sometimes if you are
hated by the right people.

Miles Franklin

The first historic images of astronaut Neil Armstrong setting foot on the moon on 21 July 1969 were beamed around the globe from NASA's Honeysuckle Creek Tracking Station, near Canberra. The events of 21 July and Honeysuckle Creek's involvement were dramatised in the film *The Dish*.

To understand the
stars would spoil
their appearance.

Patrick White, *Voss*

The better you know
yourself, the better you
know the rest of the world.

Toni Collette

Some people are born
to fatness. Others
have to get there.

Les Murray

Australia has to be a country which has the 'Welcome' sign out.

Paul Keating

Don't worry about the
world coming to an
end today. It's already
tomorrow in Australia.

Charles M. Schulz

Basically it's just
a whole bunch of
blokes standing
around scratching
themselves.

Kathy Lette on cricket

Australia is an outdoor
country. People only
go inside to use the
toilet. And that's only a
recent development.

**Barry Humphries aka
Dame Edna Everage**

You got to try and
reach for the stars
or try and achieve
the unreachable.

Cathy Freeman

Megafauna fossils have been found in Australia, including hippo-like creatures, three-metre-tall kangaroos and six-metre-long lizards. The megafauna mysteriously became extinct around 13,000 years ago, after humans arrived on the scene. Nowadays the largest indigenous land animal is the red kangaroo – although a newborn joey is only one centimetre long.

We know we cannot
live in the past but the
past lives in us.

Charles Perkins

There is nothing
so awful it can't
be shared.

Christine Lister,
The Hidden Journey

In Australia, we cling
on to whatever culture
we have. We're such a
multicultural country.

Brenton Thwaites

We cannot own the land. We are but the custodians of the land.

**Oodgeroo of the tribe Noonuccal
aka Kath Walker**

I'm always one time
zone behind myself.

Eric Bana

I'm happy to commute.
A day on a plane.
Come on. It's easy.

Geoffrey Rush

My memories are inside me – they're not things or a place – I can take them anywhere.

Olivia Newton-John

Despite camels not being native animals, Australia now has the largest wild camel population in the world. Harry was the first camel to set hoof on Australian soil in 1840, the sole survivor of several camels shipped in from the Canary Islands. Thousands of camels were transported to the outback from Palestine and India. Nowadays Australia exports camels to Saudi Arabia, generally for meat production.

It is not that I fear death;
I fear it as little as to
drink a cup of tea.

Ned Kelly

If it moves, shoot
it. If it doesn't,
chop it down.

Bush saying

Australia is so cool
that it's hard to
even know where to
start describing it.

Mary-Kate Olsen

I'm sure that there are places in the deserts in Australia that could be similar to where we might want to go on Mars.

Buzz Aldrin

Some sunshine is good for the soul, but I always make sure I wear a big hat.

Miranda Kerr

Stop worrying. No
one gets out of
this world alive.

Clive James

God made the
Harbour... but Satan
made Sydney.

Mark Twain, *More Tramps Abroad*

It's rare that there's a
role that requires an
Australian accent.

Heath Ledger

Kylie and Narelle are girls' names
that have their roots in the Aboriginal
world. 'Kylie' is a corruption of
either 'kirli' or 'karli'. Both are
words for 'boomerang' in the
language of two Aboriginal tribes.
'Narelle' could be a contraction
of Narellan, the Sydney suburb,
which was named by the Tharawal,
Gandangara or Darug peoples.

The cricket bat
is mightier than
the pen and the
sword combined.

Anonymous

Growing up on a farm was the best. I remember loving that expanse of space.

Abbie Cornish

This is the land of
dreamings, a land
of wide horizons
and secret places.

Hetti Perkins

In football, if you are
standing still, you're
going backwards fast.

Jack Gibson on rugby league

Music is a good place
to go when you're
feeling a bit down.

Archie Roach

An insect with a shell on its back which has crawled out from under a log.

Walter Bunning on the Sydney Opera House

I don't sing for anybody.
I wouldn't sing for
the Queen, dear.

Joan Sutherland

Any time you're
near a kangaroo,
it's a close call.

Jerry O'Connell

If you go out for a big night
and by some misadventure
you end up in a prison
cell, you can count on your
best friend to bail you out,
but your best mate will
be in there beside you.

Australian saying

Emus and kangaroos are very
rarely seen walking backwards,
and this is famously one of the
reasons that they were chosen for
the Australian coat of arms – they
symbolise a nation moving forward.

At the going down of the sun
and in the morning
We will remember them.

Laurence Binyon, the 'Ode of Remembrance' from 'For the Fallen', which is read at RSL commemoration services on Anzac Day

It's always good to
win a Test match.

Ricky Ponting

Aboriginal people
are either freshwater,
saltwater or desert mob.

Shari Sebbens

No one goes to
the toilet in novels.
You'd think none of
us had bladders.

Germaine Greer

Your wife is always right.
Very simple. I think I'm
going to get it tattooed
on my forehead.

Hugh Jackman

Well, Andrew Strauss is
certainly an optimist – he's
come out wearing sunblock.

Australian commentator on
the fifth Test of the 5–0 series
whitewash in 2006–07

You can impress an
Australian with a city,
but you can't impress
them with a beach.

Rose Byrne

Early explorers hankered to find the centre of the continent and, because 'centre' can be defined differently, there are several contenders. The Lambert Gravitational Centre (S 25° 36.607 E 134° 21.288) was given an unofficial thumbs up. Head south from Alice Springs, look out for the mini version of the flagpole atop Commonwealth Parliament House and you are at the centre of Australia.

I love a good barbie.

Isla Fisher

You can't drive into
the future if you're
looking into a rear-
vision mirror.

Catherine DeVrye

I'm a very proud Australian,
always bragging about
our country wherever
I am in the world.

Kylie Minogue

Australia will always be home. I sound like the Qantas ad, don't I?

Alice Englert

We are all visitors
to this time, this
place. We are just
passing through.

Aboriginal proverb

If you're interested in finding out more
about our books, find us on Facebook at
Summersdale Publishers and follow us on
Twitter at **@Summersdale**.

www.summersdale.com

KEEP CALM FOR AUSSIES

KEEP CALM FOR AUSSIES

KEEP CALM FOR AUSSIES

KEEP CALM FOR AUSSIES

KEEP CALM FOR AUSSIES

KEEP CALM FOR AUSSIES

KEEP CALM FOR AUSSIES

KEEP CALM FOR AUSSIES
KEEP CALM FOR AUSSIES
KEEP CALM FOR AUSSIES
KEEP CALM FOR AUSSIES
KEEP CALM FOR AUSSIES
KEEP CALM FOR AUSSIES
KEEP CALM FOR AUSSIES